An AMA Management Briefing

Investment Recovery

IRVING ALTMAN
PETER BAIARDI
ATTILIO BISIO

amacom
A Division of American Management Associations

Library of Congress Cataloging in Publication Data

Altman, Irving.
Investment recovery.

Bibliography: p. 42
1. Surplus industrial property. I. Baiardi, Peter, joint author. II. Bisio, Attilio, joint author. III. Title.
HD69.S9A37 658.1'55 76-26926
ISBN 0-8144-2196-2

This Management Briefing has been distributed to all members enrolled in the Finance Division of the American Management Associations. A limited supply of extra copies is available at $5.00 a copy for AMA members, $7.50 for nonmembers.

First Printing

Contents

About the Authors

IRVING ALTMAN is an investment recovery consultant with ISR, Inc. He has been associated with Stauffer Chemical Company in numerous design engineering and construction management positions. Mr. Altman was also the manager of Stauffer's Investment Recovery (Surplus Equipment) Division.

PETER BAIARDI is Program Group Manager of the General Management Division of American Management Associations. He developed and programmed AMA's first Investment Recovery seminar in April 1974. Mr. Baiardi has worked as a project manager in the construction industry.

ATTILIO BISIO is a senior engineering associate with the Corporate Research Laboratory of Exxon Research and Engineering Company. He has been Director of Engineering, Fibers Division, FMC and Manager, Elastomers and Plastics Division, Exxon Engineering. Mr. Bisio is also an adjunct professor of marketing at Kean College in Union, New Jersey.

A brief bibliography of relevant literature is also included. In addition, as noted in the report, some additional materials are available free from the authors.*

Acknowledgments

Preparation of this management briefing has benefited considerably from the thoughts and experiences of the individuals who participated in AMA's Investment Recovery Seminar. The benefits to be gained result from their contributions; the errors are the authors'.

SPEAKERS

R. D. Anderson, American Appraisal Co.
J. P. Crilly, Exxon Research and Engineering Co.
R. Maas, Price Waterhouse & Co.
K. M. Miller, Consultant
W. W. Moore II, Rohm & Haas Co.

PARTICIPANTS

J. E. Condon, Shell Oil Co.
Dennis Griffith, Continental Oil Co.
C. F. Hall, Celanese Corp.
R. H. Kelly, Tremco Inc.
Dr. J. E. Knap, Union Carbide Corp.
Philip M. Larkin, Howard Johnson Co.
Robert B. McLean, National Gypsum Co.
Dan Mapes, Kaiser Industries Corp.
John Ritchie, Consolidated Papers, Inc.
Gary Thompson, SCM Corp.
T. N. Weed, Sun Oil Co.
Walter Wojack, Ohio Transformer Corp.

Our special thanks to Jack Crilly, Roland Maas, Jim Knap, and John Condon for permitting us to use their ideas.

*Requests for this material should be addressed to Attilio Bisio, Exxon Research and Engineering Company, P. O. Box 45, Linden, NJ 07036. With the request send a self-addressed No. 97, size 10 x 13 envelope with 26¢ in postage on it.

[illegible]

Acknowledgments

Preparation of this [illegible] [illegible] [illegible] [illegible] [illegible] [illegible] [illegible] [illegible] [illegible] [illegible] [illegible] and the authors.

[illegible]

Introduction

In the course of conducting their day-to-day business, companies find that they have things—chemicals, paper, fibers, office equipment, machinery, plant equipment, whatever—that they no longer need. *Investment recovery* is an *organized* program for the recovery (reuse or disposal) of this *idle* equipment and materials. The key words are *idle* and *organized*.

Investment recovery is an important component of financial management often overlooked during the past boom and rapid growth years. Many companies never realized the tremendous value of their surplus stocks and equipment. Today, with the continuing prospect of short supplies and tight money, companies are looking to investment recovery as a way to realize new profits and improve operations. Surveys by the authors indicate that about 10 percent of the *Fortune* 500 companies have some organized approach toward investment recovery, although there are only about 15 well-organized investment recovery departments.

Investment recovery began about ten years ago in the chemical and oil industries. Until recently, the number of companies handling investment recovery as a separate function has been quite small. Now, however, the number of companies setting up or considering formal programs to sell or make further use of surplus materials has increased dramatically. Many have been encouraged by the results of concerns such as Union Carbide that regained roughly $11 million in 1974, half from sales to outsiders and the remainder from putting surplus stocks and equipment to work within the company.

Union Carbide, which established a two-man investment recovery department 12 years ago, currently has 23 people involved in this function. Among other activities, the group puts out a monthly catalog. DuPont sold $8 million of surplus equipment in 1974, while ALCOA recovered assets worth over $6 million. All companies who start investment recovery departments find that the initial returns are significantly higher than past performance in the disposal of surplus would indicate. FMC, General Foods, and Shell have all found their initial programs to be quite attractive and rewarding. General Foods, for example, earned $700,000 in the first year of its program by selling discontinued products and surplus materials, some of which would previously have been destroyed.

Scope of Briefing Paper

AMA held its first seminar on investment recovery in April, 1974. This briefing attempts to place the overall field in perspective for those companies who are considering investment recovery. Obviously, it is *not* a "how to do it" manual. However, it provides sufficient information to determine whether a program would be attractive and how to go about setting it up. Getting a program underway will require the use of expert assistance, as well as visits to those companies already active in the field.

The principles of investment recovery are quite old and well-known to all of us. Those who have held a garage sale have engaged in one aspect of investment recovery—direct sale of unwanted household goods to other consumers. Similarly, then, all companies engage at some time in the disposal of unwanted goods. For a limited number, such as car rental and leasing companies, successful disposal of surplus is critical to the overall profitability of the business. However, most companies carry out disposal on a piecemeal basis as the need arises.

This briefing addresses itself to the following areas, all of which are important for an organized program:

- Reasons for an investment recovery program
- Basic management considerations
- Size and structure of the organization
- The critical who, what, and how questions
- Making materials and equipment surplus
- Cost basis of internal transfer
- Outside sale
- Demolition
- Contract remanufacturing
- Legal and tax considerations
- Economics of surplus disposal
- Public attitudes, real and potential

1
Reasons for an Investment Recovery Program

Investment recovery must be reactive to the basic business line organization. An *organized* program works to keep down stocks, looks for alternative uses within the company, and finally, seeks disposal outside the company on the best terms. Whether the program involves one man or a small department, the emphasis is the same: making sales and providing service on surplus at the lowest possible total cost and within the time frame necessary to make the service meaningful to the conduct of company business.

An investment recovery program assists the business line organization by:

—Removing from the investment base of the product line all capital assets declared surplus, thereby improving the appropriate financial parameter.

—Recovering working capital through disposal of inventories, stores, spare parts, raw materials, products in process, off-grade finished goods, and byproducts.

—Lowering product costs through the selling of byproducts and off-grade materials, thereby generating a credit to manufacturing rather than debits in terms of warehousing costs, haulage and disposal fees.

—Increasing income through the sale of obsolete products to the secondary market rather than letting them sit in a warehouse or paying for their disposal.

—Establishing another interface, between the company and its customers through the sale of surplus.

—Eliminating production bottlenecks through the availability of an inventory of surplus property for replacement or breakdowns.

—Reducing project costs through locating good surplus for capital projects.

—Reclaiming real estate for other uses.

—Acquiring local goodwill by selling reasonably or donating surplus assets to communities, schools, colleges, hospitals, or charitable organizations.

As a business outgrows its processes, equipment, and facilities, an investment recovery program assists in the planning of new facilities through developing appraisals and estimates for the reuse, divesting, and disposition of corporate assets. When one begins to plan for a facility change, considering the investment recovery aspects can only improve the plan.

While we have made continued reference to "surplus" being involved in investment recovery, a recapitulation of the materials typically handled may be helpful:

Equipment or machines
Stores and inventory (e.g., spare parts, chemicals, catalysts and feedstocks, containers)
Scrap (productions and demolition)
Waste products or residue
Buildings
Land

The disposal of buildings and land presents unique problems and characteristics. This is a highly specialized area and is not considered in this briefing.

One may think that the list is too broad even after the deletion of buildings and land. But consider an actual list of materials that a major chemical company successfully disposed of during 1975.

Steel barrels and fiber drums
Burlap, paper, and plastic bags
Ferrous and nonferrous scrap metals
Excess inventory of new raw materials
Off-grade materials
Automobiles
Office machines and furniture
Paper—tab cards, mixed office waste
Pallets
Firearms
Plastic sheets, molding powder, and film
Textile equipment
Contaminated solvents
Catalysts
Precious metals
Instruments
Pumps
Construction supplies
Pipe, valves, fittings
Electrical supplies
Storeroom spare parts

Such a mixed bag of items is not at all atypical. Internal reuse for some of this material is clearly possible. For the others, one's imagination and creativity must be allowed to run wild. The polyethylene industry, for example, owes an everlasting tribute to the man who invented the hula hoop made from scrap and off-spec polyethylene. He not only solved a monumental surplus problem but, at the same time, made money for the companies involved. Old railroad spikes are almost worthless in the scrap market, but spend a few cents to gold plate them, and they become valuable paperweights. Ingenuity and imagination, then, are the key to the successful disposal of some items.

Often in considering whether or not to establish an investment recovery program, surveys are undertaken to determine the nature and extent of potential surplus items within a plant, division, or company. In conducting the surveys, one should recognize that surplus materials have quite specific and different characteristics. Also, the possession and segregation of surplus materials involve costs. Our studies show that these costs can amount to 20-25 percent annually of the present value of the equipment. And this estimate allows only a nominal interest charge rather than a true capital charge (see Chapter 5, "The Economics of Surplus Utilization and Disposal"). Holding on to something for possible use can be costly.

Moreover, the value of the surplus material is related to the new use, not to the cost basis. For example, an item may have value even if its direct cost identity has been lost or if the item is totally depreciated. Also, it is possible to transfer surplus within a company at less than the tax book value, although this is not often done. Finally, some items may have costs associated only with their disposal. Demolition and dismantlement, for example, lead to debris that can be disposed of only through processing and land filling at some charge.

The income generated through the program is related to how the surplus is disposed of. Maximum income will be obtained if the surplus can be reused within the company. Obviously, this is only imputed income, since it results from avoiding additional expenditures. Similarly, the least income (and in some cases a cost) results if an item must be destroyed. A rough listing of possible alternatives in decreasing order of potential income attainable follows.

Item is reused (transferred) within the company in
as is, reconditioned, or modified condition
Item is returned to supplier
Item is sold to another company
Item is sold to a dealer
Item is scrapped and sold
Item is destroyed (may be used as fuel)

Depending on circumstances, the last three alternatives listed can result in costs. Even when items are returned to a supplier, the restocking charges can run 10-25 percent of the original cost. Thus, the major effort in an investment recovery program must be devoted to reuse of surplus within the company.

Investment recovery programs are often undertaken after some disastrous experience (as discovered by hindsight) in the disposal of a facility that has become obsolete. One major oil company, for example, started a rather significant investment recovery program only after shutting down and disposing of a large production site through outside sale without looking at the alternatives. Later information indicated that a minimum of several million dollars had been lost over the next best alternative.

Hopefully, this does not happen too often and the recovery program comes about through a logical analysis of existing practices and policies of the company. Some of the key questions in such an analysis are:

- —Is there available a centralized, up-to-date surplus goods (capital) listing?
- —Are the disposal costs known?
- —Is the information about outside sales of surplus property centrally recorded and in a retrievable form?
- —Are scrap sales subjected to review by headquarters on a regular basis?
- —Are surplus items regularly used in capital programs?
- —Are the economics of capital-property disposal understood throughout the organization?

If the answer to a substantial number of these questions is "no," as it often is, then your company probably has an excellent opportunity for investment recovery, particularly if company sales are in excess of $50 million a year. A detailed analysis would probably show sufficient incentive to employ at least one person full time for the disposal of surplus materials.

2 Basic Management Considerations

The basic considerations in setting up an investment recovery program are quite similar to any new activity—clear lines of responsibility, a basis for evaluation of the program, development of procedures, and so on. However, two other considerations are quite different: (1) Controls need to be provided to minimize loss or the opportunity for collusion without excessive paperwork being involved; (2) Legal authority must be vested in subordinates for nonroutine sales transactions with outside parties.

Nothing is more embarrassing or damaging to a new investment recovery program than to find, after selling surplus material to an outside party, that the transaction cannot be consummated until time-consuming internal activities have taken place. Generally, corporate bylaws or, more often, corporate practice make the sale of items not part of the regular business line subject to extensive review and approval. Proper delegation of that authority to the investment recovery group within clearly established guidelines is essential to a successful program.

The key to a successful investment recovery program without excessive paperwork is the selection of a trusted employee of some stature and experience with the company to head it. This is no place for the new employee, regardless of his apparent qualifications. Even after careful selection, the control systems that are established and the degree of authority to be vested in the individual remain as important problems.

Since value, particularly where outside sales are involved, is so uncertain and ill defined, there is no question that opportunities for collusion can and do exist. More important, however, is that such opportunities are often suspected to exist when there are none and when none should be suspected. Therefore, an active and vigilant audit program is a necessary part of any investment recovery function, as much to protect the individual employees involved as to protect the company.

Organization—Size and Structure

Typically, the size of investment recovery groups is quite small because they are groups of trained and experienced specialists assisting operating line divisions. Many of the day-to-day activities involved in an investment recovery function are handled by the operating divisions through personnel assigned as needed on part-time basis to the investment recovery group. The role of the investment recovery group is primarily coordinative and consultive with only limited, direct responsibilities. For example, in outside sales, the investment recovery group will generally set price and make the sale, but the operating division where the equipment is located will handle the visits of potential purchasers and ship the surplus item.

Our surveys indicate that the size of the staff involved in investment recovery at the *Fortune* 500 companies ranges from two to over 20 people. The primary criteria in determining the size of the staff are the total sales volume (internal and external) and the dollar value of the outside sales. As outside sales increase, the number can grow quite quickly. Typical organization size in relation to sales volume is as follows:

Total Sales Volume (Inside and Outside)	*Total Staff (All Full-Time Personnel)*
$ 2-3 million	2-5
5-10 million	5-10
15-20 million	10-20+

The number of professionals involved in such an organization, even for the larger staffs, rarely exceeds five. If costs are to be kept within reasonable limits, the day-to-day tasks associated with investment recovery must be delegated to local units. However, the number of professionals can increase substantially if many demolition jobs are to be undertaken over a short time span. Demolition jobs are quite time consuming for the investment recovery group requiring considerable attention from experienced, skilled professionals.

Our studies and experience favor a central organization for an investment recovery program. The skilled and experienced personnel required for the program are not available in large numbers. Most of them have learned through doing while setting up a recovery program. Moreover, an investment recovery group rarely will grow larger than previously indicated, except in unusual circumstances.

As expertise in investment recovery increases throughout an organization, more direct responsibilities can be assigned to local units. Therefore, at any given time a hierarchy of groups will be involved in investment recovery within a company. The nature of that hierarchy is shaped by circumstances specific to a company.

Investment recovery programs can be located in any one of the following departments or areas of a company: manufacturing, engineering, purchasing, or corporate staff (finance, controllers, treasurers). Our studies indicate that investment recovery groups are predominantly located in purchasing departments. This is understandable in view of the historical evolution of investment recovery as a purchasing function, that is, "if someone purchased an item, he should be able to dispose of it."

Unfortunately, the skills required in investment recovery are often not developed in a purchasing department atmosphere. Moreover, the initial stages of an investment recovery program require a management overview, which is not always available to a purchasing department.

We prefer locating an investment recovery program, at least in its initial stages, as part of the corporate staff. This emphasizes the contribution that investment recovery can make to improving both the capital structure and the income performance of the corporation. In addition, follow-through on minimizing accumulation of surplus becomes much easier when operating from a corporate staff position. However, close coordination with both purchasing and engineering will be required if the program is to be successful.

The Who, What, and How Questions

We have already discussed how an investment recovery program is a program of change. Establishing the program is going to raise a number of questions. The most important of the broad questions which will need to be answered are:

- —How is the presence of surplus or obsolete material and equipment going to become known throughout the organization?
- —Who is going to collect the scrap, off-specification products, waste products, and residue from plant areas, and if required, remove them to a central location?
- —Who is going to record and store all items to be disposed of until their disposition is settled?
- —Who is going to sort (and possibly prepare) scrap, off-specification products, waste products, and residues for reuse or sale?
- —How is purchasing (and corporate engineering) going to know about the availability of surplus and equipment before order placement?
- —Who is going to handle the refurbishing of surplus materials and equipment?
- —What is going to be the basis for inside transfer and for outside disposal?
- —How are dismantlements going to be handled?
- —Who will buy used equipment from outside sources?
- —What will be the basis for sales to employees and for donations?

Developing answers to these questions will be critical. Unique answers, specific to an individual company, need to be developed. Making certain that the answers are understood and applied in day-to-day business is crucial to the success of the program.

Obviously, just how these questions are answered will directly affect the division of responsibilities among local units, purchasing, and the investment recovery group. A rather idealized division of these responsibilities is provided in Table 1.

Table 1. Idealized division of responsibilities for investment recovery.

Local Engineering and Manufacturing Units	*Local Purchasing Units*	*Investment Recovery Group*
		—Establishes guidelines for type and value of equipment to be listed —Prepares key specifications for equipment —Assists local units in evaluating idle plants and establishing disposal procedures.
Provides notification that equipment and material is surplus from idle plants, equipment left over from jobs, or dormant stock reviews	Reviews Idle Equipment Report —Determines status: capital or expense —Obtains appropriate approvals —Forwards report to Investment Recovery Group	Reviews Idle Equipment Report for completeness and significance —Adds to company master list —Adds to sales list following appropriate procedures
		Prepares periodic cumulative list of equipment and material available for transfer and sale
Reviews Idle Equipment Report for possible reuse of equipment and contacts various locations and Investment Recovery to determine possibility of reuse		
	Helps in determining economics of transfer	

Using appropriate forms and procedures, handles transfer of selected items	—Arranges for transfer and necessary accounting —Forwards a copy of the Idle Equipment Report to Investment Recovery showing receiving locations, costs, etc. (includes reuse within the plant)	—Deletes item from master list and records for statistical usage figure —Helps in transfer to plant
		Periodically reviews master list and recommends selected items be offered for sale —Prepares list of items for sale —Prepares an offer to sell on a bid basis directly to end users or dealers —Reviews bids and decides to retain, sell, or scrap
Keeps track of availability of scrap and salables and informs Purchasing and Investment Recovery	Handles local sale of scrap	Notifies local Purchasing of results of bids on scrap sales
	Arranges for local accounting	Handles sale of salables
	Notifies Investment Recovery Group of scrap sales	—Records statistics on sales and disposition figures —Prepares periodic report on sales for distribution to field locations, etc.
Obtains corporate consent for demolition		—Handles major demolition and wrecking projects —Provides assistance on minor projects

A division of responsibilities specific to the company must be established and backed up by the appropriate forms, procedures, invoices, and so on. More importantly, a user-oriented guide, stressing the economic benefits to the corporation of such a program, needs to be prepared to carry the message throughout the entire organization. Shell Oil Company and Union Carbide Corporation have prepared quite outstanding guides for use within their own organizations. A study of such guides and the development of an equivalent, better guide should be the goal of every new group. However, simply copying existing documents is not enough; the new document must be tailored to an individual organization and reflect management's thinking on just how the program should be carried out.

3
Making Materials and Equipment Surplus

The decision to declare an item—equipment, materials, stores, whatever—surplus lies with the local unit. Obviously, some materials such as byproducts, production scrap, or off-specification products become available on a repetitive basis because they are related to a specific production operation. In this case, there presumably exists some established way of disposition. However, it often can be improved upon.

The key to getting local units to declare items surplus—making them available for disposal—lies in knowing the cost to carry items for future use. The cost to carry items can be substantial. There may be one or several percentage rates, depending on whether the items have substantial differences in space requirements, insurance rates, losses, potential for obsolescence, and taxes. Insurance rates, losses, and taxes for the same item often are quite different at different locations.

The cost to carry should be built up from the individual cost elements, because these can vary if there are substantial changes in the level of items being carried. For example, if space is required to carry an item and must be rented or built, the cost of that space should be included in the cost to carry. However, if the additional space is already available and is not foreseeably going to be used to better advantage, the cost of space might not be included.

The time frame for the cost covers the period from the point the items are available to be withdrawn to the point they are withdrawn for use or to be prepared for use. Typical yearly costs to carry an item are:

Cost Element	*Percent of Book-Value Cost*
Space (heating, lighting, shelving bins, protective insurance, and systems for fire and theft)	2-5
Tending store (surveillance of stock)	6
Losses not reimbursable by insurance	3
Obsolesence	2
Taxes and Insurance	3
Cost of capital	5-15

Obviously, for equipment there may also be a depreciation charge amounting to 5-15 percent, depending upon the appropriate class life.

In addition to communicating clearly the cost to carry an item, continued management surveillance and interest will be required, at least in the early stages of the program. In some cases getting a plant to declare an item surplus is going to resemble a tug-of-war over a favorite object or relative. Some plants just like to squirrel things away for that perennial rainy day. Nothing short of a show of force is going to convince them that this is undesirable.

Fortunately, the number of groups requiring a show of force are few and far between. Obviously, the timing of when to take them on is open to considerable judgment. The best technique is simply to expose the practice without really commenting on whether it is justifiable or not. An industrial recovery program is rolling when squirreling away for the future occurs less and less.

Once an item has been recognized as being surplus, the steps involved in disposing of it are clear and simple. Most of the real work falls on the organization having the surplus because it:

—Declares equipment not in use or standby. (This reduces the plant's capital charges.)
—Fills in surplus equipment data cards (or other listing) as soon as equipment is declared surplus.
—Makes a careful, detailed, and accurate report of the nature of the surplus equipment, its condition, specifications, whether the unit is complete, and so on.
—Considers carefully the time frame permitted for disposal of the equipment.
—Provides prompt handling of transfers requested by a receiving plant.
—Informs the investment recovery group of any changes.

While many forms can be developed to smooth the way for disposal of items, sample forms found completely adequate by major chemical companies are available from the authors.

The critical question in disposal of surplus is the time frame, that is, the time limits the local operating unit places upon disposal because of some alternative need or requirement. The time frame limits the period the investment recovery group has to search for alternatives. For example, if the material is being produced as the result of a production process, there will be a continual need for disposal, and appropriate contractual arrangements will have to be developed. Obviously, for such repetitive items, contract sales are probably the best, with the contractual period being of 3-12 months duration, depending on the price volatility of the item.

Fiber barrels, for example, may be sold on a one-year contractual basis, while the sale of nonferrous scrap, such as copper, may be limited to six months. Precious materials, however, should be limited to a three-month contractual interval. While price volatility can be a critical factor in setting the contractual basis, having a dependable mode for disposal of items produced regularly as a result of a production process is the essential consideration.

The investment recovery group, in its search for alternative uses, should concentrate first on internal use unless that is obviously impossible. This may be the case, for example, for scrap and certain off-specification products. The search should be both systematic and opportunistic. Systematic means the issuance of a surplus-available report internally and then externally to potential buyers. This report should be circulated throughout the company. Reports can be universal in scope or limited to capital equipment.

In many cases the emphasis in investment recovery programs will be on improving capital budget plans. This involves a review of anticipated capital projects, engineering studies underway, and open purchase requisitions plus an in-depth knowledge of the organization, the business line, and the nature of the risk to be taken. For example, engineering must often know about the existence of surplus equipment quite early in its design studies to be able to use such equipment properly. A compressor that is made known to the engineering department at the end of six or nine months of engineering studies is almost certain not to be used. In fact, the impracticality of its use will be substantial, but if the existence of the compressor had been known to the engineering department at the start of the study, some enthusiasm about the capital dollars to be saved could have been generated.

Having located a potential internal user, the investment recovery group need only help make the transfer. Its only obligation is to be certain that the equipment is going to be used. It is essential that a receiving plant use the requested equipment. Unless it is used, surplus has merely been transferred from one portion of the corporation to another, with no overall benefit. This means that the requesting plant must have proper management authorization, such as an approved capital authorization. However, the recovery group must avoid the temptation "to play God." The first plant to request the surplus equipment gets it, unless, of course, the initial request is overruled by top management.

An investment recovery group can smooth the way for transfers by insuring that all the paperwork is handled properly. Moreover, assistance can also be extended to help in seeing that modification or reconditioning of the equipment, if required, is carried out. However, the receiving plant has the obligation to fill in a condition report. The condition report makes available information on the actual cost of the needed repairs and the state of the equipment when received.

The condition report is necessary from two points of view. One, because declaring equipment surplus reduces the capital investment of a group, it is important to make sure that unusable equipment is not pawned off on other operating divisions. Two, if there is a major discrepancy between the description of the equipment in the condition report and the original surplus equipment listing, the investment recovery group can take action. Quite often in the time interval between the listing of a piece of equipment and its delivery to a requesting plant, portions of the equipment can be removed. If this is not stopped, internal reuse of equipment will be seriously set back.

Cost Basis for Internal Transfer

The main objective of an investment recovery program is clear—to increase the use of idle or surplus equipment. Similarly, the corporate incentives for reuse are clear—savings. When a well-organized and well-directed investment recovery program is operating, money is saved in three ways:

Capital project costs are reduced.
Delivery times for capital equipment are shortened.
Income of the surplus location is increased by reducing its capital assets base.

However, internal transfer of equipment on a significant scale quickly raises the question of who pays for what. Unless properly handled, the "perceived costs" associated with an internal transfer can become an emotional issue and a stumbling block to a successful program. Even though surplus capital property is, in a corporate sense, free if internally transferred, the capital asset will become part of the receiving location's property records and be taken off those of the location that declared it surplus. There are a number of obvious possibilities for determining the cost basis of this transfer. It can be done at:

Full price
Book (depreciated) price
A value (utility) negotiated between the interested groups
Scrap value
No charge

Most companies transfer surplus property internally at the book (depreciated) price, thus avoiding possible IRS complications. (These are often more imaginary than real.) However, a few companies do permit transfer at some negotiated value less than book value; the difference between book and the utility value being shared by the two locations. The other possibilities are rarely used.

In all cases the out-of-pocket transfer costs and any repair and modification costs associated with the use of the equipment are most often paid by the receiving plant. Obviously, the allocation of costs can be suitably modified if this will encourage an investment recovery program. For example, the investment recovery group could pay for the removal of the equipment as well as the crating and shipping costs.

Supplies, spares and surplus raw materials, and all consumable items are much easier to handle. The investment recovery group can set a price which is close to current cost for similar items. This is not usually negotiable. For example, materials must move at cost or book value, whichever is lower. However, if the receiving location can prove that it can buy equivalent items locally at less than book value, the surplus items should be transferred at that price. This practice is seldom a problem because the surplus involved is generally several years old and, therefore, represents a bargain at today's prices.

A successful program of moving surplus materials requires a close watch on blanket purchase requisitions. Otherwise, one may find that stores, already in stock at one location, are being received on a regular basis at other locations. Obviously, substitutability is the key and some ingenuity may often be required. Standardization of stores between plants and the judicious use of a computer to keep track of items can help.

Outside Sale

When there is no possibility of reuse within the company, the item should be sold. Since the considerations are quite different for capital equipment, scrap items, and salables, these are considered separately.

The decision to dispose of an item should be made as early as possible, preferably before the equipment is taken out of service. Delayed action can result in the following:

Lack of money to use
Additional costs for care and preparation for storage
Increased risk of losing parts and stores
Loss of valuable information
Encouragement of gambling/speculation

Selling at the proper time while avoiding gambling or speculation is the key to successful outside sales.

Whenever possible, direct sale to the final consumer should be the goal. Not only does this lead to the best price, but it offers the possibility of repeat sales. Building up a mailing list is the key. Development of the mailing list should be supplemented by magazine and newspaper advertising and, most important, "word of mouth." The "Equipment Bulletin" from McGraw-Hill reprints the surplus and rebuilt equipment advertising appearing in its publications. This publication is quite new, but it may, in the long run, provide an inexpensive means of broadcasting the availability of equipment.

Some companies like Continental Oil Company have huge, computerized mailing lists broken down by geographical areas. Mailing lists are also available from numerous commercial sources. A specialized list for some specific item can often be developed from the appropriate trade directories. To lessen the probability of rapid obsolescence, mailing lists should be directed at particular functional titles rather than individuals.

Dealers can be used for hard-to-move items if time is an important consideration. In some cases, sales through an agent or dealer on an appropriate basis is desirable for certain very slow moving items. A clear idea of just what is being requested from an agent or dealer is the key to successful use of these services.

In looking at outside sales, a critical factor is precise knowledge of what you are selling. Too often outside sales are entered into without knowing what is being sold or what services the purchaser must render in addition to the purchase.

Knowing what you have to sell and putting it into the buyer's language is the key. Lengthy engineering specifications are of little value, but being certain that the equipment is operable means the difference between obtaining an outstanding price and a scrap price.

What you should know about capital equipment:
- Engineering specifications
- Description of condition
- Store items (spare parts) that go with equipment

What you should know about scrap and off-specification products:
- Physical nature and form
- Specifications
- Services required

Capital Equipment

When disposing of capital equipment it is desirable to sell before a shutdown because

- —Potential customers will generally pay more if they see the equipment in operation.
- —Double handling and possible damage is minimized by making shipments direct from the operations area.
- —Expense of warehouse or yard storage area is saved.
- —Deterioration and loss of auxiliary equipment is avoided.

In addition, all sorts of overtones and potential misunderstandings can be avoided.

To be able to sell equipment quickly requires a carefully worked out and agreed upon plan. The outline of such a plan is given below.

- —Fill in surplus equipment data cards as soon as equipment is declared surplus—don't procrastinate.
- —Make careful, detailed, and accurate reports of excess equipment—a good report list is the basis for recovering the full value of excess equipment, by transfer or sale. Listed equipment for transfer should have a new cost value of not less than $500 to $1,000.

List all nonproductive facilities as a unit, describing each piece fully. A complete unit can often bring top prices.

Separate reported equipment into these categories:

New: Equipment new and in excellent condition, suitable for return to manufacturer for credit.

Good: Equipment in condition suitable for transfer; that is, shipping charges and required repairs should not exceed 50 percent of the cost of similar new equipment.

Fair: Equipment not suitable for transfer but worth repairing by used equipment dealers.

Poor: Equipment not worth repairing; it should be scrapped.

When outside sales of capital equipment are made, the seller should attempt to limit potential liability arising from the reuse of the equipment. However, the seller must recognize his obligation to inform the buyer of potential deficiencies and to refuse to resell equipment that could, in his judgment, be unsafe. Since the seller loses effective control over the equipment once it has left his hands, he may have to render it nonoperable or reduce it to scrap if safety is a critical issue. (Obviously, he will then receive a scrap price.) Moreoever, complete disclosure of prior use should always be made unless it is clearly not relevant.

Outside disposal of capital equipment can be done through:

Competitive bids
Negotiated sales prices
Fixed price
An agent or dealer
Donations for use or sale

Whenever possible a competitive bidding situation should be brought about. For items such as scrap and other off-specification products that are available on a regular basis competitive bids are often utilized with some adjustment for changes in economic conditions or base prices.

Fixing a price for capital equipment is preferred by some. (Rohm & Haas has successfully followed a fixed-price policy for years.) But others let the fixed price become the basis for negotiation. Whichever policy a company follows, it must consider many elements when establishing value of surplus equipment:

Description: make, model number, size, age
Delivery time for new, similar equipment
Future maintenance and availability of parts
Desirability in the used equipment market
Condition and estimated remaining life
Special or standard type
Removal and loading costs
Time available to find a user

A wit has suggested that even after reviewing all these items and others, one should look at the ceiling to pick the price.

Scrap

The scrap salvage industry is a highly complex and fragmented industry with its own specialized terminology and client relationships. One of its characteristics is a network of informal buyer/seller relationships which have endured for long periods of time. It is almost inevitable that scrap will move to the larger dealers/wholesalers, regardless of price. There simply is no other place for it to go.

In looking at scrap, a careful distinction must be made between production and obsolescence scrap. Production scrap is of known quality and results from a manufacturing or fabrication operation on a predictable basis. Obsolescence scrap comes from dismantling plants and discarding equipment as the need arises. Production scrap is typically sold on a contract basis for terms of six to twelve months. If there is extreme market volatility, the contract terms might be reduced to three to six months or appropriate escalation clauses included.

The volatility of scrap prices and the fact that scrap prices are often quite high can prompt one to consider "gambling" in scrap. That is not an investment recovery function. Regardless of what may appear to be reports of scrap shortages and high scrap prices, the objective of the program is to move scrap at a good average return over a period of time. Sometimes through good timing, sales at the top of the market may be possible. But the maintenance of a good average price along with good relationships with potential buyers is the primary aim.

In scrap sales it is important to know exactly what you have to sell and to prevent the material from being contaminated. Segregation after contamination is often too costly to consider. With production scrap, the collection, preparation, and packaging steps are critical. Keep in mind these points:

- —Except where precious metals or other high-value materials are involved, do not attempt to segregate unless production runs produce more than several tons of a uniform composition or grade.
- —Be on the alert for possible contamination hazards from dirty containers, transfer boxes, pans, and facilities; poor procedures; improper instruction; and lack of supervision.
- —Prepare scrap as close to the source as possible.

Unfortunately, the cost of collecting low-value scrap materials, such as excess construction materials, wastepaper, and low-value solvents, may exceed potential sales revenue. The realization that some disposable scrap items have only costs associated with their handling is critical to maintaining good relationships with potential buyers.

The knowledge of the specifications and definitions used in each of the industries for each of the scrap materials under consideration is critical in obtaining a good price. Not only can confusion result if the improper definitions are used, but the unwary can fall into all sorts of traps. Obtaining in advance relevant specifications from the National Association of Recycling Industries, the National Federation of Independent Scrap Yard Dealers, and the Institute of Scrap Iron and Steel keeps one informed and helps maintain good relationships with potential buyers.

Segregation into major groups is desirable for obsolescence scrap, which is often contaminated with dirt and debris. Each major group should then be analyzed to decide whether further upgrading is possible. As a rule, however, one should not consider substantial upgrading on site. Upgrading is best done by the dealer who is going to purchase the material. In general, keep in mind these points about the collection, preparation, and packaging of obsolescence scrap:

—Some collection and segregation is mandatory, but keep it to a minimum.
—Segregate into major groups at the site during the demolition activity.
—Analyze each major grouping to decide upon the disposal technique or further segregation.
—Ship out close to the source; don't move it about.

Obsolescence scrap disposal on a major scale is a complex problem and should never be underestimated.

Having defined the scrap material, the next critical question is just what services does one want from potential purchasers. The possible number of purchasers is large. It includes local and wholesale dealers, brokers, collectors, and ultimate consumers. It is unlikely that the ultimate scrap consumer, such as a steel mill, will be a purchaser. The ultimate scrap consumer is looking for a reproducible and repeatable supply. Collectors and dealers are more likely to clean up and segregate the scrap, so if you have small quantities of scrap that have to be picked up on a regular basis, turn to a small local dealer. If you have a larger demolition job which will result in a great deal of obsolescence scrap, turn to a wholesale dealer.

The key to soliciting offers is to have a full knowledge of the material to be offered and the services required and to use the language and descriptions common to the scrap industry. Thus, when soliciting scrap offers it is important to:

—Have full knowledge of materials to be offered, including approximate quantity, known or average composition, and removal condition or services needed, such as clean up, segregation, culling, and so on.
—Know where to locate potential competitive buyers.

—Develop clear specifications, including how offers are to be submitted.
—Allow and encourage inspection. *Don't supply samples.*
—Follow up to insure that offers are received by prospective purchasers.

One should approach the scrap industry in a very cautious and conservative mood and follow through repeatedly.

Before making scrap awards, be certain to develop an independent target price using all information that is available. But be sure not to accept market quotations published in the trade journals because they are extremely misleading and often do not reflect the true competitive situation at any given time. Unfortunately, market quotations published in the trade journals and newspaper articles are often the only readily available information about scrap prices, particularly for metal scrap. They're also available to other members of management, and that can lead to the problem of unfulfilled expectations.

While the practice of selling on an assay basis is always a possibility, it is not a simple answer. Assays are only the result of the chemical analysis of a sample that represents, at most, only a small percent of the overall quantity. It is doubtful that any sample is completely representative of the material delivered, particularly if obsolescence scrap is involved. A historical record of assays reported for each class of scrap encountered in a specific business should be developed. This will enable one to spot assays which are outside the normal expectations and will result in frequent resampling.

In disposing of scrap containing precious metals, be alert to what may appear to be a small, low smelting charge expressed as a few cents per troy ounce. One cent per troy ounce is the same as $291.66 per net ton or 14.583 cents per pound.

One should follow a rather simple plan when making scrap awards.

Develop an independent target price
Put all offers on a common basis
Negotiate fairly with the bidders closest to your target price
Review all assumptions if bidders are far from the target price
Notify unsuccessful bidders
Repeat the cycle until satisfied

Salables

Just about anything a company doesn't need or want is salable. Imagination is the only limitation. Some potential salables are: inventories of discontinued products; off-specification materials; materials mixed in error; excess purchases of raw materials; overage warehouse stock; limited quantities of useful byproducts; duplicate shipments.

The list could go on and on depending what business you are engaged in. However, keep in mind the need to recognize clearly at the start those items which can be only disposed of at a cost. Developing a market for salables is basically a combination of selling and commercial development. It, therefore, requires an individual who is both a jack-of-all-trades and enterprising.

Ask yourself the following questions when you're thinking about disposing of salable items:

- —Can the material be economically upgraded to specification qualifications?
- —If the material cannot be upgraded, can it be reworked to some acceptable standard?
- —If purchased, can it be returned to the vendor?
- —Can it be used internally for some purpose?
- —With proper considerations, can it be moved through marketing for sale to established customers?
- —Can it be sold on a spot basis to that part of the business community which can't or won't buy it at posted prices?
- —Can it be sold safely to a chemical reclaimer for upgrading to an acceptable specification for subsequent sale?
- —Can it be sold to a re-seller who buys and sells in the marginal market?
- —Can it be sold to a secondary chemical broker?
- —Does it have a fuel value which can be utilized?

Disposal as waste or destruction is the final alternative for unwanted items. Disposal is becoming increasingly difficult, because land filling is not often practical, and government regulations present significant limitations on just how items can be destroyed and handled. Very often disposal or destruction results in costs, not income.

In getting rid of salables, it often pays to let the customer do the pricing. A good sharp buyer of secondary products generally knows before buying what he's going to do with the material and how much will be realized from the sales or use. Many times you will find that the buyer's price is higher than you dared hope for, and if it isn't you can always refuse or bargain upward. Unless you know the end use, you will find yourself negotiating downward.

There are certain obvious dangers connected with any business of this kind. There will always be a recurring fear that the market price for on-specification products will be affected or that secondary material will be sold either directly or through an agent to one of your accounts. Some of this will happen and is simply unavoidable. However, our experience is that it happens less often than is imagined.

Demolition—the Fine Art of Wrecking

When a number of installed items at one location become idle simultaneously, it is often economic to let out a demolition or dismantlement contract. In this way removal is done at a lower cost than you could do it, and the contractor takes some or all of his pay in scrap and salvaged machinery. In fact, the objective in a dismantlement is to have the contractor pay for the privilege of doing the job.

Dismantlement is not something to be approached in a halfhearted fashion. Careful planning, a carefully thought out contract, and a detailed work description are critical. An example of the planning that should be considered for a successful dismantlement is given below.

- —Determine future need for equipment within the company
- —If possible, obtain formal corporate agreement or consent for selling complete operating units or facilities
- —Inspect the site thoroughly
- —Estimate resale value of usable equipment
- —Estimate amount of scrap and its value
- —Estimate type of equipment and number of man-hours needed for dismantlement and removal of salvageable equipment and loading for shipping
- —Check records for specifications and amounts of equipment and materials
- —Inspect railroad siding and the truck and equipment entrances to property
- —Check plant safety rules applicable to work
- —Determine whether an air supply, fire fighting equipment, storage space, watchmen, and so on are available
- —Check to see that proprietary equipment is not included in the dismantlement and sale
- —Determine whether job will be union or nonunion
- —Determine whether riggers are needed for dismantling and removing equipment
- —Make overall estimate for job

Special contract forms are also required for dismantlement. A sample contract form is available from the authors.

About 2,400 companies specialize in wrecking and salvage according to Herbert T. Duane, Jr., a consultant who publishes the *Wrecking & Salvage Journal.* Most of the companies are small, local, and closely held, but there are two national concerns, Cleveland Wrecking Company in Cincinnati, Ohio, and Dore Wrecking Company in Kawkawlin, Michigan.

Some assistance may be required in estimating the time involved in carrying out dismantling projects and to check estimates and proposals. A simplified guide to estimating (as a function of erection time) and the maximum generally recoverable is available from the authors.

When time is of the essence in clearing out a facility, auctions can provide an excellent approach. In selecting an auctioneer, be sure that he has experience in selling the type of equipment and other materials you are offering. His experience and prior performance is a guide to his ability to attract buyers. Few buyers mean no competition and, therefore, low bids. Generally, auctioneers work closely with dealers in order to be able to appraise the equipment. Dealers also may guarantee the agreed on minimum price.

Contract Remanufacturing

Remanufacturing programs that cover valves, instruments, electronic equipment, and other equipment that needs to be reworked periodically have proven to be particularly attractive for some companies. Corporate pools of such equipment can be established and the equipment is then reconditioned to the users' specifications.

While the equipment reworking can be done with outside concerns, not all repairs are farmed out to outside shops or the original equipment manufacturer. Phillips Petroleum, for example, operates a machine reclamation center in Borger, Texas, which supplements repair shops at each of its refineries.

Quite often "make-do" decisions are in order. For example, a used 40 horsepower motor might be utilized for a job formerly done by a 30 horsepower motor. Or an old part might be reworked or tailored to fill a need, for which someone in the past would have simply purchased a new part. In some cases, one is not looking at economics, but at delivery times. Phillips has, at times, refurbished old pipe, which would have been scrapped, and used it in lower pressure applications.

Contract remanufacturing can be particularly attractive if the reworking of valves and fittings can save 50 percent of the new price, when applied to valves costing $1,000 to $5,000 new. On the other hand, for valves costing only $100 to $500 new, it is far better to scrap them. As a result of contract remanufacturing, one petroleum company has seen a $300,000 saving from reworking 1,600 valves per year.

No industrial investment recovery program, to our knowledge, presently engages in refurbishing or remanufacturing equipment for outside sale. However, various U.S. government agencies have been doing this for some time, and private companies may find it attractive in the future.

4
Legal and Tax Considerations

There are important legal, tax, and accounting considerations in an industrial recovery program. Unfortunately, it is impossible here to provide anything but broad guidelines. The remarks we make should be regarded as a bare minimum only and should be very carefully checked against the advice of a competent corporate or outside adviser.

Legal

All investment recovery involving outside parties require a sales contract which is governed by the Uniform Commercial Code (UCC), Article 2, Sales. An in-depth understanding of the terms necessary for a binding contract is essential for those involved in industrial recovery programs. Particular attention needs to be given to the avoidance of premature commitment to an incomplete contract. The contract will generally need to be in writing to be legally binding, since the sales almost always are more than $500.

Aside from the price, assuming there is agreement on what is being sold, the most important provisions to be considered in the sales contract are the warranties and disclaimers. Warranties and disclaimers are concepts used to allocate risk between the parties. It is unlikely that the contract will contain an expressed warranty, that is a statement or promise made by the seller to the buyer as to performance or suitability of an item for a specific use. If a warranty is required by the buyer, it needs special consideration because the nature of the materials and equipment involved in investment recovery makes such promises risky.

However, two warranties of quality can be imposed by law: merchantability and fitness for a particular purpose. Merchantability involves the concept that the property must be of a quality generally acceptable in the line of trade that handles the goods described in the sales agreement. Since sales of surplus recovery goods are a special case, the person making the sale is not a merchant within the meaning of the code and no warranty of merchantability should apply. However, this concept needs to be carefully reviewed when and if outside sales become a significant part of an investment recovery program.

When a particular purpose is contemplated by the buyer and this is known to the seller at the time of the contract, then the buyer may be said to rely on the seller's skill or judgment to furnish suitable goods unless properly disclaimed. There can be a warranty implied by law that the goods will be fit for the purpose. This can be particularly important if the buyer and the seller are not at all equal in size or sophistication. Therefore, it is important that any implied warranties of quality, merchantability, and fitness for a particular purpose be disclaimed. The provisions of the UCC must be precisely followed in making the disclaimer, and disclaimer language must be conspicuous.

Wherever applicable the property should always be described as "used" or "secondhand." Not only should the purchaser be permitted to examine the property he is considering for purchase, but whenever possible he should be asked to do so and, if feasible, even test it. The desirability of having a prospective purchaser see a machine in operation is obvious. Also, the words "as is," "as they stand," and "with all faults" should be used in appropriate places in the sales contract.

Jack Crilly of Exxon Research and Engineering Company has suggested for consideration the following disclaimers of warranties as meeting UCC provisions.

- —SELLER MAKES NO EXPRESS WARRANTIES WITH RESPECT TO ANY OF THE PROPERTY SOLD UNDER THIS AGREEMENT.
- —It is expressly understood and agreed that the descriptions of the property sold hereunder are for identification purposes only, and are not intended, nor shall they be construed to be, express warranties as to the condition, quality, and/or performance of the property.
- —SELLER MAKES NO WARRANTY OF MERCHANTABILITY WITH RESPECT TO THE PROPERTY SOLD UNDER THIS AGREEMENT, AND BUYERS AGREES TO TAKE THE PROPERTY "AS IS" AND WITH ALL THEIR FAULTS.
- —Buyer affirms that he has not relied on seller's skill or judgment to select or furnish goods suitable for any particular purpose, AND THE SELLER MAKES NO WARRANTY THAT THE GOODS SOLD UNDER THIS AGREEMENT ARE FIT FOR ANY PARTICULAR PURPOSE.

No statement or promise should be made regarding the conditions, quality, or performance of the property. It is particularly important that this not be done in verbal discussions between the buyers' and sellers' agents. Cautioning and instructing manufacturing personnel who may show the item to prospective buyers is critical. When a description of the property requires the inclusion of a performance quality, for example, one 1,500 KW generator, the contract should expressly provide that the description is for identification purposes only and is not intended to be a warranty of condition, quality, or performance.

If for some reason an expressed warranty is intended, that is, some specific warranty is going to be made, it should be drafted with the utmost care. Legal advice is absolutely necessary. As a minimum, the expressed warranty should be given in place of all other warranties of quality, including, but not limited to, warranties of merchantability and fitness for a particular purpose. The parties to a surplus sales transaction are permitted to limit their liability under the provisions of the UCC. Sellers are advised to take advantage of this risk-reducing mechanism by including carefully drafted clauses limiting the time in which suit may be brought to a period not greater than one year and the amount that may be recovered as well as specifying that it will be the purchaser's exclusive remedy.

Tax Guidelines

Disposal of surplus property requires an understanding of our changing tax laws and federal depreciation rules. To aid in getting the best recovery, the use and advice of corporate law, tax, and accounting departments are essential. Only broad generalizations are given in our discussion.

The tax accounting treatment of asset retirements is a complex subcategory of tax depreciation. The complexity begins from the existence of three different sets of asset retirement rules:

—The Class Life Asset Depreciation Range (ADR) System, if elected, for assets placed in service in 1971 or thereafter.
—The Guideline Class Life System, if elected, for assets placed in service in 1970 or prior years.
—Facts and Circumstances Depreciation if the Class Life ADR System or the Guideline Class System has not been elected.

The tax accounting rules that govern an asset retirement are generally determined when the asset was acquired and not upon retirement or disposal. Moreover, the rules are quite specifically outlined by the Treasury Department, and in most circumstances there is only limited leeway.

When multiple asset accounts are used, there is no recognition of gain or loss upon retirement of the asset if the retirement is ordinary. Since investment recovery does *not* for our purposes involve land, most of the retirement will be ordinary. (Exceptions are casualty retirements and major retirements of the assets in an account.) All proceeds, gains, and losses are added to the depreciation reserve of the multiple asset account. Gains are recognized only if the depreciation reserve exceeds the cost basis. This is not likely to occur often.

For item accounts, since the retirement closes the account, gains and losses are recognized to the extent of the difference between the cost basis and the depreciation reserve. Moreover, the cost of dismantling, demolishing, or removing assets in an item account is deductible as a current expense. Asset retirements under Facts and Circumstances Depreciation are subject to a complex set of rules and are not a unified system.

What can we make of all this besides seeking expert counsel? The economic elements of decisions on disposal of capital assets come in pairs as can be seen in the following lists.

Cash Recovery	*Income*	*Taxes*
cash income	scrap income	ordinary
tax savings	sales income	capital gain

These elements combine in different ways depending upon the age of the assets and the applicable regulations.

To begin with the decision should revolve around the cash income—the larger the cash income, generally, the better the deal. This will always be the case for items purchased after 1971 and placed in Class Life ADR multiple accounts.

For item accounts or items purchased before 1970, the nature of the loss incurred for items *not* fully depreciated (a common case) is critical. This is because the tax consequences are different depending on whether the item is sold as a used asset or as scrap. Some rules of thumb follow:

—If the capital item cannot be sold for more than 25 percent of net book value, transfer it to a Scrap and Salvage Account. Scrap it and take the benefit of the loss.
—If the asset has a significant scrap value, sale as a used asset must return over 50 percent of net book value to be attractive.
—For fully depreciated items, the disposal decision is best based on cash income. Capital gains may result if it is not.

In certain cases, any losses will have to be amortized over the average useful life of the asset, not the remaining years.

Capital equipment can be transferred between locations within a company at any mutually agreed price. This will *not* impact or modify the depreciation status of the overall company. Unfortunately, transfers at anything but the book value can become a football game between the departments involved, with the investment recovery group being caught in the middle. Moreover, the documentation needs to be first-rate and thorough so that the best tax status category can be determined.

Roland Maas of Price Waterhouse has suggested the following ideas for planning purposes when considering a retirement program:

—Accelerate loss recognition by placing assets to be retired early in separate accounts.
—Combine large numbers of assets into one account to maximize deferral period on gains.
—Consider what the likely pattern of retirements will be before choosing depreciation methods.
—Choose the manner of retiring assets carefully by considering the possible advantages of sale versus trade-in or abandonment versus sale.

—Time retirements from plant closings to occur in a single year.
—Retire assets through use of scrap or supplies accounts.
—Avoid sales of assets between affiliated corporations that file consolidated returns.
—Consider using several asset accounts to permit additional retirements to be treated as extraordinary.

In addition, when new equipment for which federal investment tax credits have been obtained is scrapped, recapture of the credit in whole or part may be possible. If this looks possible, a review with the appropriate specialists is in order.

Tax Free Trade-in

The trade-in of surplus equipment for similar (preferably identical) new equipment can offer economic advantages over the normal route of disposal of used equipment followed by purchase of new. The exchange is free of federal tax implications and often state and local sales taxes. The normal disposal/purchase transactions result in a tax obligation that is the difference between the tax on the disposal incomes plus any others that are applicable and the depreciation tax credit on the new equipment. However, the advantage of the tax-free trade will depend on both the age of the asset and whether the Federal Investment Tax Credit is in force or not. Generally, the older the asset, the more advantageous the trade-in. This also minimizes the possibility of significant tax credit recapture.

Federal Investment Tax Credit	*Advantage of Tax-Free Exchange as a % of Value Exchanged*
In Force	0-10
Not in Force	5-15

However, trade-ins may not qualify for some state or local financing, such as Pennsylvania's Peter Fund.

Donations

Donations can be advantageous, compared to sale, only if certain conditions are satisfied. The fair market value (replacement cost or retail price) must exceed the sum of the net book value and the total depreciation taken for tax purposes since 1961. Also, the fair market value must exceed the normal sales value (price that a dealer would pay intending to resell it at a higher price). To minimize possibilities of later difficulties, the item must be:

Declared surplus
Listed internally as available for transfer
Advertised for outside sale
Valuable in its present form to the recipient

In addition, the item must have a recorded cost and book value. The administrative costs and difficulties associated with the clearing and substantiating of charitable contributions are considerable. One should not attempt to get a federal income tax deduction unless the sales value is at least $10,000.

5 The Economics of Surplus Utilization and Disposal

The alternatives for handling idle equipment and materials need to be evaluated from an economic decision-making point of view. These alternatives are:

Reuse at the same location
Transfer to another location
Disposal—sell, exchange, or donate

If there is a potential use within the company, the major uncertainty that must be evaluated is when the item will be used. Unfortunately, the answer to this question is often determined at any given location in relative isolation. When surplus assets are considered in a corporate context, the possibility of use should be significantly increased. Therefore, the elapsed time until a surplus asset is again in use should be reduced.

Reuse of existing assets avoids the alternative of outside purchase at a higher cost. However, the timing of reuse is often not clear. (We exclude those corporate locations which have well-deserved reputations as "pack rats.") The choice to be made is between selling the surplus asset and buying a new one when needed or retaining the asset and reconditioning it when needed. The probability of use at a future time is inherent in the problem of maximizing the expected discounted cash income under conditions of uncertainty.

Figures 1, 2, and 3 present relationships between estimated probability of use and the possible economic parameters involved in making a disposal/retain decision. A number of specific assumptions obviously enter into these figures, although such assumptions can easily be modified. (The specific bases and assumptions for these figures are available from the authors.)

With Figure 1, if the approximate sales income and reconditioning costs are known, the minimum probability of use required within a chosen time period can be determined. This will be a break-even probability making the economics of sell/buy new equal to retain/recondition. If the estimated probability of use within the time period is less than the break-even probability, the asset should be sold.

Generally, the sales value of used assets is in the low range, roughly about 20-30 percent of new cost. Reconditioning costs typically are in the range of 20-50 percent of new cost. Therefore, if the probability of use over a reasonable time period is less than 50-80 percent, the assets should be sold.

Figures 2 and 3 can assist in the analysis of sell-retain economics when there is an *absolute certainty* that the asset will be used. The maximum allowable reconditioning expense is significantly influenced by both sales value and when the item will be needed. If the reconditioning expense exceeds 50 percent of new cost, it will be difficult to justify carrying an item more than a year. Moreover, a realistic appraisal of cost to carry, as is done in Figure 3, will generally limit the hold period to less than three years. Retaining an asset for future use without having some specific use in mind is sinful!

Figure 1. Probability of use of surplus capital equipment.

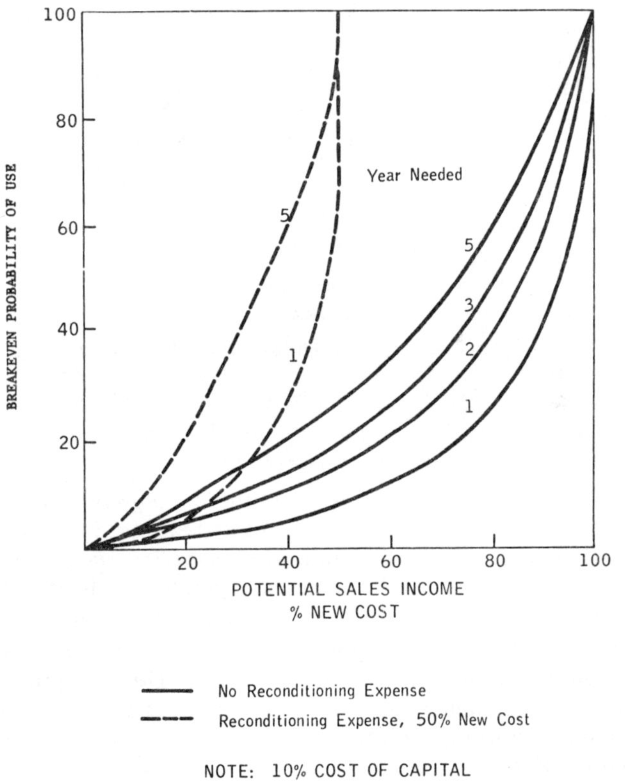

Figure 2. Reconditioning expense of surplus capital equipment (no cost to carry).

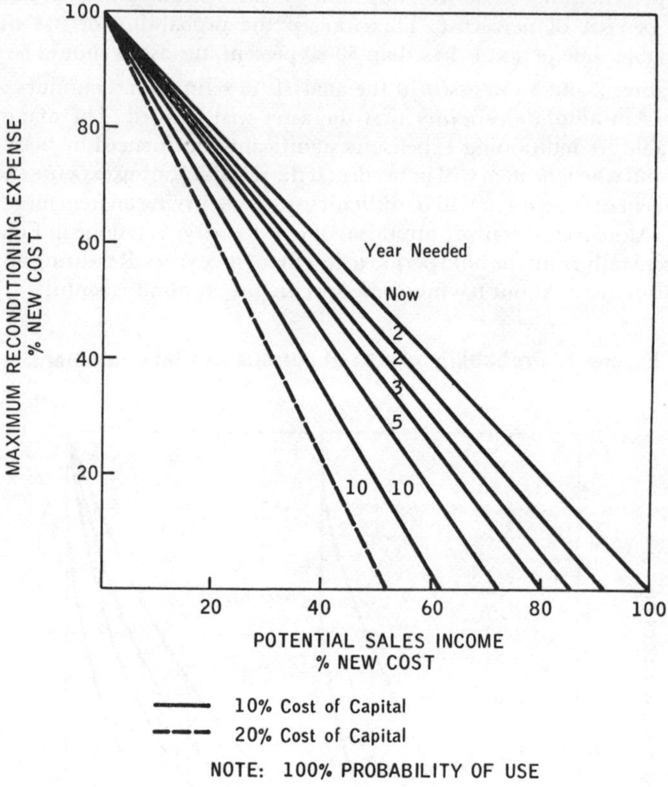

Public Attitude Toward Investment Recovery

Although affluence and the throw-away attitude are everywhere evident, the people of the United States still largely subscribe to the "waste not, want not" adage. It is not possible to determine whether this is nostalgic lip service or concrete belief. What little evidence we have points to both ways at once, and the picture is muddled by the emergence of ecology as a household word.

Overall, the behavior of the public is clearly contradictory and it is difficult to form a conclusion about public attitudes. However, one can feel confident that a corporate program directed at investment recovery will be well received by the public and considered part of the frugal experience that we all should share.

Figure 3. Reconditioning expense of surplus capital equipment (10% cost of capital, 10% per year cost to carry).

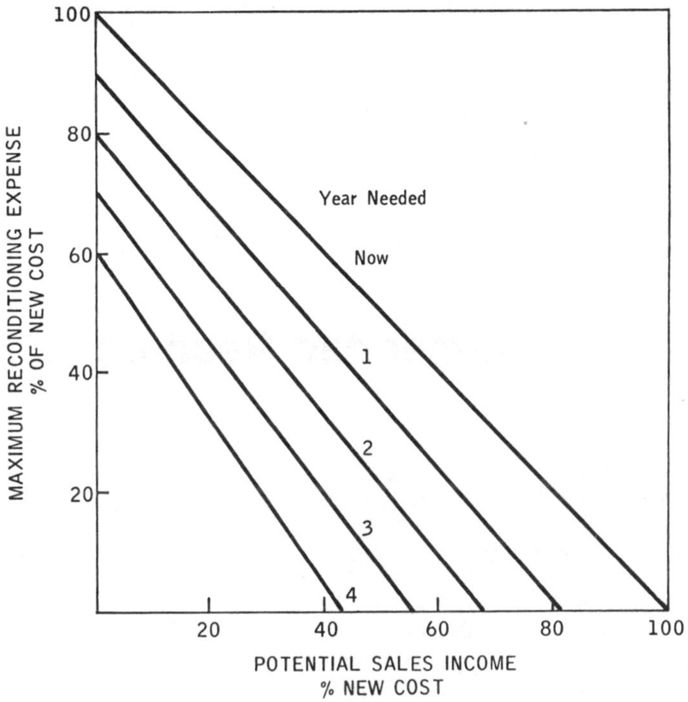

NOTE: 100% PROBABILITY OF USE

Recommended Readings

General

Darney, A. and Franklin, W.E., *Salvage Markets for Materials in Solid Wastes,* EPA-SW-29c, PB-214 152/1, 1972.

Hayes, R.H., "New Emphasis on Divestment Opportunities," *Harvard Business Review,* Vol. 50, No. 4 (1972): 54-64.

Hillman, R.H., "How to Redeploy Assets," *Harvard Business Review,* Vol. 49, No. 6 (1971): 95-104.

Hilton, P., "Divestiture: The Strategic Move on the Corporate Chessboard," *Management Review,* Vol. 61, No. 3 (1972): 16-19.

Resources Recovery Bibliography, National Center for Resources Recovery, Inc., Washington, D.C., 1974.

Vignola, L., Jr., *Strategic Divestment,* AMA, 1974.

Demolition

Breiner, M.B., "Business Techniques and Plant Demolition," *Chemical Engineering Progress,* Vol. 68, No. 3 (1972): 78-79.

Culham, W.B., "Construction and Demolition Debris Need Special Care," *Solid Wastes Management,* Vol. 18, No. 6 (1975): 50-52.

Kolbe, R.A., "Industrial Auctions: Bargain Hunters' Paradise," *Purchasing*, Vol. 79, No. 3 (1975): 41-45.

Law, D.J., "How to Manage a Plant Demolition Project," *Plant Engineering*, Vol. 29, No. 7 (1975): 61-63.

Economics of Surplus Disposal

Barnes, T.M., *Summary Report on Impact of Railroad Freight Rates on the Recycling of Ferrous Scrap*, Institute of Scrap Iron and Steel, Inc., Washington, D.C., 1972.

Bierman, H., Jr. and Smidt, S., *The Capital Budgeting Decision*, New York: Macmillan, 1975.

Blake, A.B., "The Asset Disposal Decision," *Chemtech*, May 1975, pp. 282-286.

Salables

Battelle Columbus Labs, Ohio, *A Study to Identify Opportunities for Increased Solid Waste Utilization. Volume I*, EPA-SW-40D. 1-72, PB-212 729, 1972.

Belknap, M., *Paper Recycling: A Business Prospective*, Subcommittee on Solid Waste, New York Chamber of Commerce, 1972.

Economics of Recycling Waste Materials, Hearings Subcommittee on Fiscal Policy, Joint Economic Committee, Congress of the United States, Ninety-second Session, November 8-9, 1971; U.S. Government Printing Office.

Lehto, B.O., "Economic Parameters that Govern Secondary Fiber Usage," *Paper Trade Journal*, Vol. 156, No. 15 (1972): 36-37.

Milgrom, J., *Incentives for Recycling and Reuse of Plastics*, Final Report, EPA-SW-41c-72, PB 214 045/7, 1972.

Recycled Paper Products, National Association of Recycling Industries, Inc., New York, N.Y.

Recycling Resources; A Guide to Waste Utilization, National Association of Recycling Industries, Inc., New York, N.Y., 1973.

Scrap

Bird, M.M., "Industrial Scrap Management: A Study of Some Current Practices," *Journal of Purchasing*, Vol. 7, No. 1 (1971): 41-47.

Effective Technology for Recycling Metal, National Association of Recycling Industries, Inc., New York, N.Y., 1971.

Gordon, R.L., Lambo, W.A., and Schenk, G.H.K., *Effective Systems of Scrap Utilization: Copper, Aluminum and Nickel,* Bureau of Mines-OFR-18-72, PB-210 795, 1972.

Gordon, R.L., Schenk, G.H.K., and Lambo, W.A., *The Collection of Non-ferrous Scrap: A Literature Review of the Copper and Aluminum Sectors,* Bureau of Mines-OFR-18-72, PB 210 833, 1972.

Operations in the Non-ferrous Scraps Metal Industry, National Association of Recycling Industries, Inc., New York, N.Y., 1973.

Recycling Lead in the United States, National Association of Recycling Industries, Inc., New York, N.Y., 1973.

Wright, R.E., "Scrap: How to Get the Top Dollar," *Purchasing Magazine,* Vol. 63, No. 11 (1967): 60-61.

Surplus Equipment

Epstein, J.P., "Disposing of Surplus Equipment," *Chemical Engineering Progress,* Vol. 68, No. 3 (1972): 80-81.

"New Look at Old Equipment," *Chemical Week,* Vol. 93, No. 13 (1963): 49-50.